INTRODUCTION

This booklet is not concerned with a specific ethical question in the way the other booklets in this series are. It is concerned with the way in which the Bible may be used in ethical discussions amongst Christians. It is therefore a discussion about an authority and the interpretation of that authority in ethics.

People use the Bible in ethical discussions in a great variety of ways. No doubt you have heard someone say that when he was pondering some difficult ethical decision a verse of the Bible came to him, as if by inspiration, and he made his decision according to what the verse 'said' to him. If you listen to Christians talking about ethical matters, or read books by Christians about ethics, then you will quickly see that the Bible is used in all sorts of ways. Sometimes it is used in a completely indiscriminate way, without any regard for the kind of literature that is being quoted, or the place and time within which the quotation arises. That kind of indiscriminate use of the Bible is fairly obviously unfair to the Bible itself.

There is another kind of indiscriminate use of the Bible which is also unfair to the Bible itself, and that is the way in which people use pieces of the Bible from very different parts of it without any concern for the whole picture. In ethical discussions a typical instance is the use of something in the Old Testament without regard to its place in the developing biblical pictures of the truth.

Some people shy away from the idea of development in the Bible. In some ways it is true that parts of the Old Testament are not substantially changed by the later biblical tradition. But if we believe that Jesus fulfilled the Old Testament in any sense, then we have to be prepared to see not only continuity in the Bible, but also discontinuity. Jesus did change some things.

It is this particular part of the question of the use of the Bible in ethics with which I am here concerned in this booklet. What is the inner relationship between the different parts of the Bible for the purposes of ethics? The discussion that follows is very much an introductory discussion, and is intended to raise some of the issues for further consideration, perhaps in church discussion groups, house meetings or seminars.

There is a further emphasis in this booklet. It is particularly interested in questions of social ethics. This is partly because questions of social ethics are of special importance to us today, and partly because the use of the Bible in discussion of social ethics is more difficult and raises a number of problems in an acute way. One of those problems is the relevance of the social structures of Israel in the Old Testament for the Christian in the modern world.

3

Two interests therefore explain the emphases in this booklet. On the one hand the question of the inner relationship between the different parts of the Bible and in particular the question of development within the Bible, and on the other hand the concern for questions of social ethics and thus the problem of the relevance of the social structures of Old Testament Israel.

There are no final solutions contained in this booklet. It is an introductory discussion to open up the questions. I hope it may also prove to be a useful guide towards some answers.

Bruce Kaye
August 1976

BIBLIOGRAPHICAL NOTE

It is not easy to suggest books which are relevant to the theme of this booklet and which might be used for further reading. There are not many books which deal with this subject directly, and I have found that in coming to the point of view which is argued in this booklet I have drawn on ideas learned from other disciplines such as sociology and legal philosophy, as well as the main-line Biblical and theological works. The following list is one of the books I have found myself referring to in the course of writing. The books marked with an asterisk might be regarded as ones to start with.

Abrahams, G. Morality and Law, London 1971.

Braaten, C. E. Eschatology and Ethics, Minneapolis, 1974.

*Bruce, F. F. This is That, Exeter, 1968.

Buber, M. The Kingship of God,

*H. von Campenhausen, Tradition and Life in the Church, London, 1968

*Cullmann, O. Salvation in History, London, 1967

Daube, D. The New Testament and Rabbinic Judaism, New York, 1973

Davies, W. D. The Gospel and the Land, Berkeley, 1974

De Vaux, R. Ancient Israel, London, 1961

Ellis, E. E., Paul's Use of the Old Testament, Edinburgh, 1957

Gärtner, B. The Temple and the Community in Qumran and the New Testament, Cambridge, 1965

Ginsberg, M. On Justice in Society, Harmondsworth, 1965

Käsemann, E. New Testament Questions of To-day, London, 1967

Manson, T. W. Ethics and the Gospel, London, 1960

*Manson, W. Jesus and the Christian, London, 1967

Niebuhr, R. An Interpretation of Christian Ethics, London, 1936

van Oyen, H. Ethik des Alten Testaments, Gütersloh, 1967

Perrin, N. The Kingdom of God in the Teaching of Jesus, London, 1963

Pound, R. Law and Morals, New York, 1969

von Rad, G. Old Testament Theology, Edinburgh and London, 1962

Schlier, H. The Relevance of the New Testament, London, 1967

*Schofield, J. N. Law Prophets and Writings, London,

Stone, J. The Province and Function of Law, Sydney, 1946.

Wilson, S. G. The Gentiles and the Gentiles Mission in Luke-Acts, Cambridge, 1973

the Bible
in Ethics

by

Bruce Kaye

Senior Tutor, St. John's College, Durham

GROVE BOOKS

BRAMCOT

CONTENTS

First Impression September 1976

Second Impression May 1979

ISSN 0305 4241

ISBN 0 901710 97 0

1. THE OLD TESTAMENT AND ISRAEL

A. The Historical and Covenantal Framework

The old Testament is basically a book about the people of Israel. It is about the way in which God called to himself a people for his own possession. The people were bound to God by his covenant and God bound himself to them by his covenant-keeping love. The covenant is the way in which God's relations with men are explained. The fundamental covenant is that established at the time of the Exodus. God delivered Israel from Egypt and brought her to a land of promise. The covenant and the land bring into existence the nation as a people of God. Israel saw this covenant as quite in line with God's dealings with the Patriarchs, and indeed with mankind in general after the flood. The covenant with Abraham is first expressed in brief form in Genesis 12.1-3, but then repeated in more detail in Genesis 15 and 17. In Genesis 15 we have first of all the promise to Abraham, a statement of what God has done ('I am the Lord who brought you from Ur of the Chaldeans, to give you this land to possess' Gen. 15.7), and then the sealing of the covenant (Gen. 15.8-21). In chapter 17 there is first of all the basic transaction (Gen. 17.1-8), then the giving of circumcision as the sign of the covenant (Gen. 17.9-14) and the giving of the promise of a child (Gen. 17.15-21).

The centrally important Exodus covenant is much more fully described in Exodus 19-24 and Deuteronomy 1-11. In Exodus we have a statement of what God has done and what he requires, the agreement of the people and elders, instructions about the preparation of the people, further preparations on the day of the sealing of the covenant, the declaration of the covenant (Ex. 20.1-17), the fear of the people, the re-assertion of the religious character of the covenantal obligations, further elaboration in terms of case law and then the ceremony of sealing the covenant (Ex. 24.1-8).

In 2 Samuel 7 there is some variation from the preceding patterns of covenant. This covenant is with David the king and his descendants and the account begins with David's response to what God has done, a correction of Nathan's agreement and then the surprisingly unconditioned promises of God (2 Sam 7.8-17). These are preceded by a recitation of what God has done, a promise of what he will do in relation to the people and to David, and then a delivery of the terms of the promises to David.

The covenant in each case is based on what God has done. This quite naturally is less specific in the Abrahamic covenants in comparison with the Exodus and Davidic covenants. The foundational Exodus covenant, however, is incomprehensible without a clear understanding of its basis in the mighty act of deliverance by God of Israel from Egypt. In this sense it is clear that grace precedes and is the basis of the obligations, the law. The terms of the covenant ('you shall be my people, I will be your God') are religious, and state the obligations for the parties involved. Obedience on the part of the people, and loving provision on the part of God.

5

It has often been noted that this covenant pattern is similar to the pattern of Near-Eastern Treaties of the time, treaties, between a great king and a lesser king (cf Joshua 12). There are common terms such as 'own possession', 'to go after other (gods)', 'to love', 'to fear', 'to sin', 'to hearken to his voice', 'to do as he commands', and there are similarities in the actual form used. However, there is no preamble with the King's titles in the Old Testament covenant, nor is there a list of Gods witnessing the covenant. There is in the Exodus covenant a summing up which is not found in the contemporary patterns:

	Ex.	Deut.
Historical prologue	20.2	1-3
Stipulations	20.3-23.19	4-26
A document clause	—	27
Blessings and curses (these are in the reverse order to the normal pattern)	24.20-22	28
Summing up	23.23-33	29-30

The historical basis of the covenant is God's merciful deliverance rather than the conquest of the great King in the treaty. This covenantal way of conceiving of God's dealings with Israel has certain implications. The law is emphatically the personal demand of a sovereign God from his people (cf. Deut 4.32f.). Therefore justice in Israel is to parallel God's justice, indeed it is to be his justice (cf. Deut. 10.17ff., and Lev. 20.26; Israel is to 'be holy for I the Lord am holy').

The law is given by God to and for the people. It is not given by the king, as in Mesopotamia, and the king is subject to the law like everyone else (Deut. 29.18ff.). Thus a legal offence is really a sin in the framework of God's relationship with Israel. God is in the midst of the social regulations, and offence against a fellow Israelite in the terms of the covenant is an offence against God. Thus what we might think of as religious and moral or legal obligations are found all together—we might even say indiscriminately (e.g. Ex. 22.14-31). Because every Israelite is responsible under this 'mixed' or 'total' law, the law must be taught to everyone (Deut. 6.4-9). Punishment for offences in such a context can be quite easily understood as a purging of the evil from the midst of the society (cf. Deut. 21.1-9). The covenant pattern shows that Israel is bound to God and under his law as a nation.

It was inevitable that with the settlement in Canaan the social institutions of Israel should undergo changes and developments. However these developments have a theological significance as well as being of sociological interest. They have theological significance because of the covenant and because Israel saw itself, in that covenant, as ruled by God. Israel was a theocracy.

The coming of the kingdom introduces new and foreign ideas and practices into Israel, and was for some an apostasy from the special position of Israel as the covenant people of God. The account in 1 Samuel 8 is worth noting in a little detail. The first three chapters of the book are taken up with the relationship between Samuel and Eli, and then chapters 4-7.14 with the successful wars of Israel against the Philistines while Samuel was judging the people. 2 Sam. 7.15-8.3 summarizes Samuel's itinerant work as a judge during the more peaceful times after the wars and shows how his sons, like Eli's sons before them, did not share their father's integrity, but became corrupt and offensive to the people. Thus in 1 Sam. 8.4 all the elders of Israel gather together and bring on behalf of the people a request that Samuel give them a king to govern them, as in all the nations. Samuel was displeased with this request and in his prayer he receives an answer from God. The answer is very significant. The request is not a rejection of Samuel, it is a rejection of God. It is a rebellion against the covenant, against God's theocratic rule in the covenant community. This rejection, or apostasy, is consistent with the sinfulness of the people; ever since the deliverance from Egypt they have forsaken Jehovah and served other gods, that is, they have continually broken the terms of the covenant. Nonetheless the request is to be acceded to, on condition that they understand the terrible ways of kings, in contrast to the kindly ways of Jehovah. The people persist in their request despite this warning, and so they are handed over to the consequences of their sin. The granting of a king to Israel is God's judgment on Israel for its rebellion and apostasy (compare Rom. 1.24).

This way of seeing the coming of the kingdom in Israel is reflected also in the traditions about the charismatic saviours in the book of Judges. Gideon, for example, refuses to become a king because Jehovah is the ruler of Israel (Jdg, 8.22ff.). Similarly the story of Jothan (Jdg. 9.8ff.) shows a complete repudiation of monarchy. The complete devotion of the Nazarites to Jehovah (Jdg. 14.5, 7; 16.16) and the presence of the Rechabites (Jer. 45.6ff) also are signs of opposition to the new institution of the monarchy.

However, it would be a mistake to think that the monarchy did not gain religious acceptance in Israel. It is, in fact, quite remarkable that the transition to national and monarchical institutions from the older clan structure of Israelite society was achieved so quickly and without an acute crisis of faith. The fact that Saul was really a charismatic leader in the first instance may have helped, just as disillusion with the older order as reflected in 1 Samuel 1-3 probably made a change more acceptable. It is noteworthy that David did not trespass on traditional roles, or sacred places, thus avoiding conflict with the older conservative traditions.

The new order of things implied major changes in the social structure and the religious outlook in Israel. The kingship of David is endorsed on practical grounds first of all—ties of blood, and his military prowess—and only in a confirmatory way is he king by God's designation (2 Sam. 5.1-3). The establishment of Jerusalem as his residence between the two major groupings in Israel is his own action and achievement, and thus it comes to be known as the city of David. The time of David's kingship was also one of strength and prosperity. A royal court of distinction coupled with intellectual and religious advances also helped to establish the new order.

Three important confirmations of the kingship helped to give the monarchy some acceptance within the traditional faith of Israel. First there was the confirmation of David's kingship by Nathan's prophecy (2 Sam. 7) and, secondly, the temple was built and it was built on crown land (2 Sam. 24.24ff.). The later tradition of Zion being the mountain of God where he had his dwelling place confirmed the position of the temple and Jerusalem (Pss., 78.68ff.; 46; 48; 76). Thirdly, the bringing of the ark of the covenant from Shiloh to Jerusalem, was of special importance because it linked David's kingship with the old clan traditions.

All this, however, must not cloud the fact that throughout the history of Israel the monarchy had an uneasy relationship with the older traditions of faith in Jehovah. This comes out in the attitude taken to David's census in 2 Samuel 24 which was so clearly contrary to the old tribal and charismatic disorganization. It can also be seen in the continuing prophetic criticism of the temple, the cult and the nation. This is especially true in the eighth century and following, when there is an external threat to Israel. The prophets look into the future and see doom for the nation. That doom is the judgment by God on Israel's sin (e.g. Mic. 1.2-5). The prophets, of course, look beyond the doom and judgment to a new work of God, a new salvation for Israel and the nations which will be different from, and superior to the political and national order of their day.

B. The Ethical Material
There is, of course, a great deal of ethical material in the Old Testament, and it is not my intention to survey this material here. A great deal of it has to do with the moral responsibilities of the individual, and the use and interpretation of this material can be pursued in much the same way as similar material in the New Testament. However, from the point of view of understanding the relationship between the different parts of the Bible for the purposes of properly using the Bible in ethics, there are two questions which we must consider. First the matter of the large amount of ethical material in the Old Testament which is directly related to the social and political structures of Israel; this is what we may call the legislative material. The other matter is the development in the Old Testament of the belief in God as creator. The creation material is of significance for ethical discussion because it portrays images and values relating to man in general.

The legislative material can be distinguished because it is part of the national structure of the covenant because it has coercive sanctions. In the period of the kingdom the law of the King is very clearly legislation for the nation. Because the law material in this context is set within the framework of the covenant it presumes a national commitment to Jehovah, and thus a national obligation. It is not just that every individual in the nation has himself personally and individually accepted an obligation to obey God's law, though that sense is there to some extent. Rather it is the case that the nation as a whole is committed to God's law. The fabric and structure of the nation is expressed in God's law. This can be put the other way around. God's law is in this material clearly to be understood as God's law, or God's will, in legislative form. It is a statement of God's will for a redeemed nation in terms of legislation for that nation.

The legislative material not only compromises moral absolutes and ideals because it has to deal with the realities of the social situation for which it is legislated, but it also involves some arbitrariness in its administration. The law, as law, cannot cover every possibility, and those who administer it are willy-nilly involved in applying to concrete particular situations the arbitary generalities of the legislation Deuteronomy 24 allows for the moral compromise of divorce because it has to cater for the realities of the social situation covered by the legislation. However, the compromise is held in check; a man may not re-marry his divorced wife if she has subsequently been married to someone else. Such a thing would defile the land, to which the nation was bound by the promise and provision of Jehovah. The instruction not to do any work on the Sabbath is an example of an arbitrary rule which calls in particular circumstances for interpretative application.

The legislative material in the Old Testament also contains much that is concerned with the maintenance of the cult which symbolized the covenant. This is true of the Mosaic covenant particularly, since the cultus of the monarchy is later and less formulated.

These three characteristics of the legal material in the Old Testament must affect our understanding of the way the material is to be used for ethical purposes. In the first instance they affect the way we understand the morals, or moral values which are embodied in this legislation, and then, secondly, they affect the way we might seek to relate the moral values embodied in the legal material to any discussion of Christian ethics, because they are intimately related to a socio-political order which is not carried over into Christianity. The three conditioning factors are therefore of great importance, and bear repeating. The legal material is part of the covenant of a redeemed nation and therefore it presupposes a national commitment to God's will. Because it is legislation it has the characteristics of law; that is to say it contains arbitrariness and compromise. Thirdly, it contains a lot of cult material which is of only indirect value for moral discussions.

Besides the legal material there is also a wealth of material which can be regarded as expressing moral values and is of more direct interest in moral discussions. The decalogue (with some questions about the law of the Sabbath) is one good example of this material. The material, however, is conditioned by the fact that it is set within the tradition of Israel. A good example of this is the laws about slavery. Within Israel the institution of slavery hardly existed because of the terms upon which Israelites could keep fellow Israelites as slaves. The terms were so severe that slavery virtually did not exist. This is almost certainly due to the influence upon the social laws of the understanding of the deliverance of the people from Egypt as a redemption, a buying back from slavery. Because they were once slaves in Egypt, the Israelites are to treat their slaves well. Because they were set free from the slavery of Egypt, they are to set their fellows free from slavery. This national self-understanding conditioned the social structure. It did not, of course, affect quite so much the question of Israelites enslaving foreigners.

Behind the various moral rules and judgments to be found in the Old Testament are values about man and his moral character. One of the great achievements of the Israelites was to come to an understanding of their God not just as the deliverer in this or that particular situation or episode, but as the lord of history who guides the affairs of men and nations everywhere. It is a further achievement of the faith of Israel that this belief was brought into relationship with the natural world. Jehovah was not just the deliverer of Israel, but he was also lord of the nations. And he was not just lord of the nations now, but in the past and in the future as well. Furthermore, and more daringly, he was not only lord of history in the affairs of men, but he was also lord of the natural world within which man lived—he was Creator. This process of projection carries important implications for ethical discussions because the ethical values that are carried through to this confession of Jehovah as creator are less historically and nationally conditioned in their expression. We might almost think of the creation material as 'de-contextualized' covenant material.

The connexion between the creation story and the pre-history of Israel draws attention to certain ways in which the creation story is to be understood. The present order experienced by the faithful Israelite whose confession is embodied in the Genesis story is a 'fallen' one. The reality which he experiences is that of disorder, enmity, toil and death. Everything is definitely no 'very good'. On the contrary, he survives by the sweat of his brow and the pain of childbirth. The faith of the redeemed, however, looks beyond this disorder. The ambiguity of the present situation is accounted for by the claim that behind the distortions and evil there is order, behind the enmity there is harmony and relationship, behind the toil there is ease and sustenance and, behind death there is life. It is there, and not here, that the 'very good' is to be found.

Three important implications flow from this confession within the faith of Israel. First, it means that there is both continuity and discontinuity between the present situation and the very good situation of paradise. There is discontinuity in that murder, arrogance and sexual vices are not present there. However in this paradise there is work and marriage, which are elements in the present situation.

Secondly it emphasizes that the faith of the redeemed is one of hope. The style of the Genesis story casts the picture in such a way that suggests a chronological order to the events. However, the emergence of this belief in Israel in relation to a belief in the lordship of Jehovah over history, his judgment upon Israel by the process of historical developments, and of a hope in a new and better salvation in the future means that we must also see this picture of 'paradise lost' as also a picture of 'paradise yet to be given'. Because the belief in God as creator is so rooted in the redemptive experience and faith of Israel it must always be seen in that perspective. We may not in fairness detach the one from the other.

Thirdly, the belief that God is lord over and in history means that the nations of the earth may not be excluded from the providence of God. The Israelite may not therefore become exclusive in his attitude towards the nations, even though the nations do not share Israel's common commitment to Jehovah.

10

In this brief review of the ethical material in the Old Testament I have suggested that a distinction needs to be made between the legislative material and that material which more directly expresses moral values. I have also tried to highlight the significance of the creation traditions in relation to moral values.

C. The Use of the Ethical Material

Certain limitations and difficulties in the use of the legal material in the Old Testament have already been mentioned; the presupposition of a holy nation, the material's character as legislation, and the large amount of cultic regulations. By the time we come to the end of the Old Testament major historical and theological changes begin to emerge. The land is despoiled by the Assyrians and the Babylonians, the nation is in ruins, David's throne is gone and his heir is in captivity. The temple also stands in ruins. The judgment foreseen by the prophets has come to pass, and the future is not clearly discerned. There are lines of hope expressed in the imagery of the past, but the holy nation and its divine institutions are gone. The sad and pathetic situation faced by Ezra and Nehemiah, their bitter attempt to enforce exclusive moral standards as arbitrary legal requirements, such as in marriage, only serve to highlight the momentous change that has taken place.

It is true that the temple, and Jerusalem are eventually rebuilt, and the redevelopment of a nation begins, and comes to fruition after a fashion. However, we will have to come into the New Testament to see how the holy nation and the land, the kingdom, and the temple are interpreted.

The more general moral material is not subject to the same historical and theological judgment. Here we have a picture of individual moral values for life in society. The material is historically and socially located. In order to make use of it we need to identify the underlying values that are expressed in the particular expressions and relate them to our own situations and our own values as Christians. The concern of the Old Testament moral material is with man's response to God's activity and character. This picture is not always drawn in the same way, and one Old Testament scholar has said that in the Old Testament there is no consistent picture or evaluation of man. If we are content to leave the matter in a very general form at the moment we will see shortly that the New Testament has the same basic concern of man responding to God's activity and character. However in the New Testament the picture is more clear, and more precise.

2. THE NEW TESTAMENT AND CHRIST

After the event, and with the benefit not only of the New Testament itself, but also of a long history of Christian interpretation, it is very easy for us to affirm that the Old Testament hopes and expectations are fulfilled in Jesus Christ. However, the New Testament shows us that the early disciples had quite a bit of trouble understanding precisely how Jesus saw himself as fulfilling the Old Testament. They plainly did not understand how it was necessary, according to the scriptures, for the Christ to suffer many things and to be rejected by the elders and to rise again on the third day. We have the advantage of seeing the matter in the light of their hard-won understanding.

A. The Old Testament Structures and Institutions

The land of promise which was so important in the Old Testament, and in later Judaism, seems to disappear completely from view for the New Testament writers. There is heavy irony in John's words when he records the chief priests and Pharisees gathering the Council together and saying 'What are we to do? For this man performs many signs. If we let him go on thus, every one will believe in him, and the Romans will come and destroy both our holy place and our nation.' (John 11.47ff.). The thought of the nation being replaced is reflected also in the parable of the wicked husbandmen in Mark 12.1-11, which the Jewish leaders perceive as being directed against them.

This point can be further illustrated by the way in which Paul uses the Old Testament ideas about inheritance. In the Old Testament the basic conception goes back to the promise given by God to Abraham in Genesis 12.7, 'To your descendants I will give this land'. This promise is alluded to later in the Old Testament, and the land is referred to as the 'land of the fathers'. The Rabbis and the apocalyptic literature reflect a more transcendent idea of inheritance, so that the Book of Jubilees can speak of inheriting the whole earth, and the Psalms of Solomon inheriting eternal life. Paul does speak occasionally of an inheritance in the future which is something like a reward for serving Christ here, or the destiny of those who belong to Christ in the resurrection. However, the really important thing in Paul is that Christ is now the focus for the inheritance. The true inheritor of the promise of the land is Christ, and those who share that inheritance with him do so because they belong to him, and not because they have earned something by their 'works', nor because of anything about themselves individually apart from Christ (Gal. 3-4). In Romans 8 Paul speaks of Christians as children of God and heirs of God and fellow heirs with Christ. In both Gal. 3 and Rom. 4 the idea of inheritance carries with it the thought that salvation now includes the gentiles. Not only is the land as inheritance transformed, but the national prerogatives of Israel are gone.

What is true of the land and the nation is especially true of the temple. In Acts 7 Stephen calls upon the prophetic tradition in the Old Testament which regarded the temple as a mistake from the beginning; the Most High does not dwell in houses made with hands. The most characteristic New Testament interpretation of the temple, however, is that it has been replaced by Jesus.

12

As God's presence amongst his people had been seen in the temple, now his presence is to be found in Jesus. In John's gospel Jesus clears the money-changers out of the temple and declares that they should not make his Father's house a place of trade. That could have been the action of a zealous Jew, but John's account goes on with a discussion about the authority on which Jesus had removed these people. He declares he will restore the destroyed temple in three days, and John specifically interprets this statement of Jesus as a reference to Jesus' own body and to his resurrection. The risen Christ will actually replace the Temple. Thus God is present with his people in their relationship with Jesus, not by the institutions of Judaism or by anything else. 'If a man loves me, he will keep my word, and my Father will love him, and we will come to him and make our home with him.' (John 14.23 compare Mt. 18.20).

There is a further development of the temple imagery in Paul. He draws an analogy between the temple and the body of the Christian individual in order to emphasize that the Christian's bodily actions should be holy and reflect the character and will of God (1 Cor. 6.19).

However, he also speaks of the Christian group as a temple (2 Cor. 6.16). In this sense the Christian group is where God is present. This is in line with his understanding that the Christian group meets in the name of Christ, and is not far distant from Mt. 18.20, 'where two or three are gathered together in my name, there am I in the midst of them.' God is present with his people in the person of Jesus, in his life, death and resurrection. His continuing presence is not tied to any place or location, it is where Christians gather in the name of Jesus.

As with land, nation and temple, so also with kingdom, the New Testament transforms the conception. It is startling that the kingdom is so central a motif in the teaching of Jesus, and the origins of Jesus' ideas have been much discussed by scholars. Many have drawn attention to similarities between some of Jesus' sayings about the kingdom and references in the apocalyptic literature. It is not easy to be certain about the ideas of Jesus' background, though the background given in the infancy narratives is less political than perhaps the popular ideas, and more related to the previous tradition of prophetic hope within Israel.

This is a circle in which the prayer in the Eighteen Benedictions would fit; 'Bring back our judges as at first, and our rulers as aforetime, and be thou King over us, O Lord, thou alone.' The kingdom in this, and most other contexts, in the literature of late Judaism, is thought of as the rule of God, which is the sort of thing intended by the Rabbis when submission to the Torah is 'to take upon oneself the kingdom (or rule) of heaven.' When the kingdom is thought of as the personal rule of God then it is easier to understand statements in the gospels which refer to entering the kingdom, seeking the kingdom, looking for and receiving the kingdom. It is also the way to understand Jesus' charge that the Pharisees by their rules and traditions shut the kingdom to seekers. It is clear in Jesus' teaching that the individual can now enter the kingdom, and that that same individual can look forward to a future manifestation of the kingdom. What is important here is not just that there is a present and a future element in the belief about the kingdom, but that the kingdom now is seen in Jesus himself, and that individuals come to him, belong to him, and follow him, and thus enter and are in the kingdom. The kingdom, present and future, is now personal. It is the personal rule of God in the affairs of men, and men enter it by personal commitment.

Because Jesus himself embodies and expresses the rule of God, Jesus becomes the touchstone for knowing what the kingdom is like. John's gospel makes an important emphasis which must be given full weight in our thinking. The king is most significantly seen as king in his crucifixion. This is particularly seen in John 19 where the theme is developed with a good deal of irony. In the conversation between Pilate and Jesus it is clear that Jesus' kingdom is not of this world in the way in which Pilate understands kingdom, or kingship. Jesus' kingdom is not like the monarchy which Israel wanted in 1 Samuel 8. Rather, his kingdom is characterized by his testimony to the truth. Jesus says that he has come into the world to bear witness to the truth, and everyone who is of the truth hears his voice. That is Jesus' understanding of his kingship. It is important to notice that while his kingship is not *of* this world, it is nonetheless most certainly *in* this world. His kingship is exercised by testifying to the truth and people enter his kingdom by hearing and obeying, or doing, that truth. It is also worth noting that in John's understanding the sign on the cross shows that the crucifixion most clearly declares the character of this kingdom. This kingdom is entered by faith, by obedience to the truth. There is no national barrier to the kingdom, and it is not located in any one place, nor is it co-extensive with, or to be identified with, any nation or institution.

Just as in the Old Testament Israel's faith in God led to the assertion of his lordship over all nations, not just Israel, and over the whole of creation, so too in the New Testament there are clear signs of the same projection of faith. A very good example of this is the hymn to Christ in Col. 1.15-20. In this hymn Christ is given status and honour in a general way in the creation in just the way that Israel in the Old Testament had given status and honour to God.

In this hymn, however, the perspective is not that the world is seen as created, but rather that Christ is pre-eminent in the created order. The point is not that the world, and men and human society, are created, as if that were something apart from redemption in Christ. Creation is an expression of the lordship for good of the covenant God, that is to say, the redeemer God. Thus, Christ the redeemer is Lord over all, and the involvement of Christians in society, and in the world, is an involvement under the lordship. The perspective is from the Lord, and his lordship, rather than from the creature in his createdness. The focus in this theological projection is on Christ the King who is Lord of all creation.

So in Colossians, Christ is the first-born of all creation, that is, he is pre-eminent in creation. In Him all things were created of whatever kind or order or organisation; in heaven and on earth, visible and invisible, thrones or dominions or principalities or authorities, all things were created through him and for him. It is, however, significant that the hymn arises in the context from Paul's thanksgiving for the conversion and Christian life of the Colossians, and it leads to exhortations for right Christian conduct. In other words, the confession of Jesus as Lord in and over creation arises from the experience of him in redemption, and it leads to ethical obligation.

It is significant that in the rest of the letter this same Christ is the model for Christian maturity. The apparently enthusiastic religious tendencies in Colossae are countered by Paul's insistence on the centrality and pre-eminence of Christ. Union with Christ means a certain life-style. It means putting away immorality, impurity, passion, evil desire, covetousness, and, anger, wrath, malice, slander, and foul talk. On the other hand, it means putting on compassion, kindness, lowliness, meekness, patience and love.

We see then that the New Testament sees the Old Testament realities of the land, the nation, the kingdom and the temple as fulfilled in Christ. In this process, however, all these realities are given new and personal meaning. For nation and land we have God's presence in Christ and his assembled people. The kingdom is seen in the person of Jesus and in his testimony to the truth, and the kingdom is entered by obedience to the truth which Jesus brings and embodies. For the temple we have Christ and in particular the risen Christ and his presence amongst his gathered people. W. D. Davies, at the end of a long study of *The Gospel and the Land* (1974) says, 'in sum, for the holiness of place, Christianity has fundamentally, though not consistently, substituted the holiness of the Person: it has Christified holy space.' (p.368).

B. The New Situation

The coming of Christ brings a new situation for mankind. The ways of God with man are radically altered as to their form and terms. True, as always, man is to walk by faith in the mercy of God. However, the Old Testament institutions and structures are forever gone. The nation and the land and the Temple no longer have significance. God is now present in Christ and amongst his assembled people who are scattered throughout the world. The kingdom as known in David and his heirs is taken away, and now Jesus has brought the rule of God in his own person, and the risen and ascended Jesus exercises his kingly rule amongst his people by his word and his Spirit. This kingdom is completely different from the kingdoms of this world, such as that in Israel of the Old Testament. This kingdom is not of this world, though the subjects of this kingdom are still in this world.

The wiping away of the structures of the Old Testament in the New Testament is only one side of the picture. There is now a new profile. That profile is worked out with varying emphases in the New Testament, but there are five central points to it.

(i) God's saving activity is now to be seen in Jesus Christ. The life death and resurrection of Jesus of Nazareth constitutes a saving event for mankind. This piece of history is now of abiding and continuing significance for men. In it God has shown himself as our saviour. When in former times God spoke to our forefathers, he spoke in fragmentary and varied fashion through the prophets, but in this final age he has spoken to us through his Son. He is the one through whom God created the universe, the one whom God has made heir of the whole universe. He shines with the brightness of God's glory; he is the exact likeness of God's own being, and sustains the universe with his powerful word. After he had made men clean from their sins, he sat down in heaven at the right hand of the Majesty on high. (Heb. 1.1-4).

(ii) Christians are those who are related to Christ. They are his followers, they are those who believe, those who belong to Christ. As such they are not identified by location. They are scattered throughout the world. In the world, but not of it.

(iii) The risen Christ, through his Spirit continues the guiding and teaching work of Jesus. The Spirit makes contemporary the things concerning Jesus according to John's gospel, and also according to John's gospel those who have not seen Jesus and yet believe are blessed. Similarly 1 Pet. 1.8: 'without having seen him you love him; though you do not now see him you believe in him and rejoice with unutterable and exalted joy.'

(iv) Christians scattered throughout the world assemble from time to time to encourage and edify one another. They are to let the word of Christ dwell richly among them. They are to share one bread. These gatherings are the occasions on which the Christians can be seen as a church.

(v) The behaviour of Christians as they pursue their calling in the world is to be consistent with their relationship to Christ, and is thought of as a co-operating with, or participating in, God's continuing activity in the world. Thus, Paul tells the Philippians, 'work out your own salvation with fear and trembling; for God is at work in you, both to will and to work for his good pleasure.'

c. The Ethical Character of the Christian Life

There are, of course, variations in the particular emphases and the particular images used by different New Testament writers to describe the Christian life. The controlling theme throughout, however, is that the Christian is to be Christ-like. This reflects the fact that the New Testament writers are gripped by the claims of Christ and by the belief that in him God's revealing and redeeming purposes for men have come to fulfilment. We can trace this theme through various New Testament writers to show how in their different ways they are all pointing back to Christ.

The Synoptic Gospels:

Jesus appears in Galilee preaching the good news of the kingdom and calling on men to repent and believe the gospel. However the precise form of the new life which Jesus brings is quickly made apparent in his calling a band of men to follow him and be his disciples. It is not long before Mark's gospel is able to refer to different groups of people in terms of their relationship to Jesus; the disciples, those with him, those around him and those outside the band of followers. From the beginning the Christian life emerges as a question of disciple-calling. Men are called to follow Jesus, to be his disciples; that is to say, those who learn his ways and walk in them. The disciple, the learner, of Christ by following Christ comes to share Christ's life. The disciple of Jesus is a friend of the bridegroom, and it is to the disciples that the mystery of the kingdom is revealed. To those outside it is veiled and remains a secret, but to the disciples it is plainly given. Undoubtedly the initial stages of Jesus' ministry called for the development of a particular band of men—the twelve. However, the conception of the Christian life as that of a disciple or follower of Jesus was never eradicated from the thinking of the early church. The experience of the twelve in this respect is not exclusive, but it is rather typical, it is a model for all discipleship.

The disciple is called also to deny himself. That challenge is laid upon the disciples after Jesus has been confessed by them as the Son of the Living God, but it also finds expression elsewhere in the Gospels. The denial of self is the necessary inner side of the following of Jesus. There is no profit for the man who gains the whole world, his whole life, if he loses his own life. The point of this contrast is that the disciple is called to give up his commitment to his life, to deny himself. It is also significant that this challenge comes at a crucial point in Jesus' ministry—just before he sets himself to go to Jerusalem. It is also important in that in Mk. 8.34 and Lk. 9.23 this teaching on discipleship is given to everyone. Henceforth all the world is to know that this is the pattern of Christian life.

We may take this pattern a step further by reference to Mark 10. Jesus has just challenged a rich young man to deny himself, to sell all his goods and to 'come, follow me'. Lest the point be lost he then turns to the crowd and expands on the difficulty of the rich entering the kingdom of God. This challenge provokes a reaction amongst the disciples and there is a continuing discussion along these lines amongst them. James and John seek to deny themselves and to give up all in this life by seeking greatness in the kingdom of Jesus. They ask if they may sit one on either side of Jesus in his kingdom. This evokes from Jesus a powerful statement of the character of Christian discipleship. It is fundamentally following Jesus, it is also denying oneself, and now it is also seen as living according to the pattern of Jesus own life. That life-style is in sharpest contrast to the life-style of the world at large. There great ones make people feel the weight of their authority, but amongst the disciples of Jesus greatness consists in loving service. Why? Because the Son of Man came not to be served but to serve, and to give his life as a ransom for many.

Thus the picture of the Christian life as following Jesus has two elements in it. On the one hand there is the denial of self, and on the other there is the commitment to the life-style of Jesus. All the time, you will notice, we go back to Jesus, his life and teaching, as the key to our understanding of Christian life. That arises quite simply and naturally from the fact that the New Testament writers saw in Jesus the fulfilment of God's revealing and redeeming. All else fades into insignificance in the light of this man of Nazareth who lived, taught, died and rose again, and who is Lord of all.

Paul:

The perspective in Paul's letters is a little different from that in the Gospels. That is to be expected because of the different circumstances. However, the basic conception of the Christian life is strikingly similar. Paul's way of seeing the situation is a little more dynamic and he has much more thoroughly worked into this aspect of his thinking the eschatological significance of Jesus' life, death and resurrection. He thinks first and foremost of the Christian as someone in relationship with God. God is thought of by Paul as dynamic, and as moving towards his purposes of perfection. This end-perfection has been inaugurated in Christ, and the character of that end-perfection has been manifested in Christ. The Christian is thus someone who is incorporated into this movement of God.

In the relationship between God and man, God has taken the initiative, and that initiative makes possible, and leads to, the invitation to faith and commitment in the gospel. The commitment is to God in Christ, and the relationship is basically ongoing and dynamic.

God's purposes in his activity are moving towards perfection, the perfection that will, in Paul's mind, be attained in the resurrection when God is all in all. This perfection is cosmic in its scope, but as far as the individual is concerned the perfection is defined in terms of the lordship of Christ, and of the Christian's growth into the perfection of Christ. Thus Paul is able to sum up his ministry in these terms. 'Him [Christ] we proclaim, warning every man and teaching every man in all wisdom, that we may present every man perfect in Christ.' (Col. 1.28).

This end-perfection has been inaugurated by Christ. This is the already present aspect of his eschatological thinking. However, that very focussing on Christ as the inaugurator of the end-perfection carries with it the implication that the character of the end-perfection may be found in Jesus Christ. Thus, as in the Gospels, we are back with Christ as the model and example for the Christian life. Because Paul believed so strongly that the coming of Christ represented a new beginning, and a fulfilment of all that had gone before, and because he looked for the further fulfilment of this coming at Christ's return, he saw Christians as caught between the resurrection of Christ and their own resurrection. The dynamic movement to the end-perfection has been initiated in Christ's death and resurrection, and the risen Lord is active in bringing his people to this maturity. Paul takes over the Old Testament ideas of the Spirit of God and subsumes them under the controlling belief in Christ.

The Christian therefore, for Paul, is someone who, by his commitment to and union with Christ, is incorporated into the dynamic movement of God. Because this incorporation into the activity and purposes of God is seen by Paul in terms of the individual's relationship with Christ, and because Christ expresses and reveals the end-perfection towards which the Christian is growing, the Christian life is a matter of becoming more and more Christ-like. This brings us back to the example of Jesus for the disciple in the Gospels.

Other New Testament Writers:
Other New Testament writers also have this basic idea of Christian living as following Christ. 1 Peter specifically appeals to the example of Christ in his sufferings so as to encourage and direct his readers when they fall into suffering and persecution. Similarly the letter to the Hebrews makes its critical ethical appeal in chapter 12 in terms of laying aside every weight and the sin which clings so closely, and running with perseverance the race that is set before us, looking to Jesus the pioneer and perfecter of our faith.

D. The Use of the Ethical Material

The ethical material in the New Testament focusses in the first instance on the picture of Jesus as the model and example for the Christian. Not only do the apostolic writers in the New Testament offer Jesus as an example, in his life and in his incarnation (as e.g. in Phil. 2), but also the Gospels show Jesus to have been regarded in the early church as a teacher. It is true that Jesus' teaching is often very situational, and there is some doubt as to whether it can always really be intended in its own terms to have enduring and abiding application in detail. It is hardly likely that we would be persuaded that, taken as a whole, Jesus intended people to sell all their possessions, as he told the rich young man to do.

The apostles also give instructions to their readers, and a Christian moral tradition does seem to be emerging in the New Testament period. It is not the case that the new faith swept aside all formal ethical obligations and norms. From the beginning there was a clear sense of ethical value which informs the way in which love is expressed. However, it is not our task here to develop a picture of the ethical teaching of the New Testament. It is sufficient to notice here that a tradition of ethical reflection and decision making develops in the New Testament along the lines of the profile of the new situation of the Christian given just above.

It is more important for us to notice the new institutional situation of the New Testament Christians. There is no legislative material such as in the Old Testament. The state is no longer made up of the redeemed, nor is it a holy nation. There is no consideration of the state or legislation which directly deals with these matters in a general way. The references to the social institutions of the day in the New Testament are the remarks of those who simply are responding to the actualities of their situation. This is also true in regard to the internal social structure question for Christians of church order. There is no prescribed state or ecclesiastical structure in the New Testament. There is a deal of material which relates to these two questions, but the *ad hoc* character of the material must condition and restrict the general value of such references. The one exception to this in the New Testament is that there is an attempt to give a theoretical basis for the family structure which the early Christians adopted.

The interpretation and use of this ethical material is to be pursued in much the same way as with the material in the Old Testament. The particularities of the form of the material have to be clarified and the underlying values identified. In the New Testament, however, these values are more apparent and more clearly spelled out. It is worth noting that the same projection of the redeemed into the realm of the world around them, in the form of a belief about God as creator, appears also in the New Testament. Jesus is described in creation story terms and he is described as lord over the creation and the agent of God's creating.

Given that there is a similarity in the approach to be taken with the Old Testament and the New Testament, it is nonetheless very important to notice that there are some dramatic differences. The moral issues in the New Testament are more often drawn in personal terms and the inner motivation as absolute obedience to God is more strikingly important than in the Old Testament. However, the most dramatic change is the institutional framework within which the life of the believer is located, and within which he fulfills his ethical obligations. The social structure of the state and the nation as a holy nation responsible under God according to the covenant is completely swept aside in the New Testament. There is now no Christian definition of the state. The structures of the Old Testament are gone. The traditions in the Old Testament, which had given support to the coming of the monarchy and to the theological interpretation of the holiness of the nation as a whole before God, are used in only an indirect and metaphorical way in relation to the Christian group. There is no attempt to establish a Christian society or nation, and even the communalism of the early Jerusalem Christians is not copied anywhere else.

The problem for the Christian involved in society and seeking guidance on questions of social ethics is made the more difficult, if he wishes to use the New Testament, by the emphasis there on the Christian as someone cast into the world and charged to live there alongside his non-Christian neighbour, in a pluralistic society. He may not withdraw from that situation since that is where he is to work out his salvation, where he is so to live his life as before God and men that in and by that life he worships God. If the Christian uses the New Testament to help him make his ethical decisions then he will not want to try to create some kind of Christian state, nor to implement the legislative pattern of ancient Israel.

Two things can thus be said by way of conclusion. First that when the Christian uses the Bible in ethical discussion and decision-making he must read the Old Testament from the standpoint of the New Testament, he should read the New Testament in turn from the standpoint of the picture of Christ, since he is the model, the image, which he is to follow. The New Testament is least helpful in what may be called the structural questions of social ethics, and it speaks to these only indirectly and marginally. The Christian is, in this area, involved in developing a picture and approach from hints and general principles about human existence.

The second thing to be said is that the Christian is not involved in making his ethical decisions in isolation. The responsibility for his decisions and actions is his and his alone, but he is a member of a Christian community; a group, whose function is to enable its members to grow in maturity, to grow up into Christ. That maturity involves being able to discern what is significant, to be sound in judgment. The church as a living community, an assembly on the way to maturity, is thus crucial to the Christian's ethical decision-making. For the modern Christian this is not something that is restricted to ethical matters. The interpretation of the Bible is a central part of the whole life of the Christian church.